ENDORSEMENTS

"*Words from My Father* grabs you and won't let go. Arethia Rinfrow takes you on a journey with her. She does not hide from the reader the secret places most people hesitate to share. Tears to triumph, despair to victory, searching to finding—it's all here.

I met Arethia many years ago as she was writing and producing plays throughout our area. Her works always had a powerful message that left you thinking about life's possibilities. I noticed that she was remarkably humble and full of faith. Her infectious smile never hinted at the cobbled path she had traveled. This book increases my appreciation of her as an awesome woman of God.

Words from My Father is a mix of strong poetical imagery and spiritual insights that you will not want to put down. "Well done, my friend!"

— Dr. Deborah Coulter Ivey
First Lady, Beulah Baptist Church
Cincinnati, OH

WORDS FROM MY FATHER

IN THE BEGINNING WAS THE WORD

Arethia Hornsby Rinfrow

GOOD FEET PUBLISHING
CINCINNATI OHIO

WORDS FROM MY FATHER
Copyright © 2016 by Arethia Rinfrow.

arinfrow@yahoo.com

Scripture taken from the New King James Version®. Copyright © 1982 by Thomas Nelson. Used by permission. All rights reserved. Sermon notes from Pastor Tracy Ventus used by permission. All rights reserved.

Cover photo by Jonathan Hornsby of Blulense.com
Line editing by Dr. Cheri Westmoreland
Copy editing by Sally Hanan of Inksnatcher.com
Book Layout ©2013 BookDesignTemplates.com

Ordering Information:
Quantity sales: Special discounts are available on quantity purchases by corporations, associations, and others. For details, contact the "Special Sales Department" at the address above.

Words from My Father/Arethia Rinfrow.—1st ed. March 2016
ISBN 978-0692-64840-7
Good Feet Publishing, Cincinnati, Ohio

This book is dedicated to my brother, Norman Hornsby III. He was the most awesome brother God could have given me. There are no words to express the loss of his presence in my life. He is now my angel.

Contents

FOREWORD

As I read the words in this book, I was captured by how real and true the words rang out. I know Arethia's story, and in this book she totally bares her heart and soul to her readers.

I have counseled her through some of her hurt and the pain of her horrible past, but now I see a woman walking in freedom, beauty, and victory over the ashes and ugliness of yesterday.

God has miraculously healed and delivered her out of the bondage and darkness of what happened to her. Now I believe God is going to use the words in this book to come alive in her readers' spirit and soul, and they are going to work a great healing in many people's souls.

I believe that if we, the readers, take in her words, which are God's words of healing to hurting souls, God will allow us to receive healing for our souls too. I believe that this is God's purpose for this book.

So let the healing begin—as you read this book and take the journey to the healing of your soul.

— Pastor Tracy E. Ventus,
New Mission Missionary Baptist Church
Cincinnati, Ohio

INTRODUCTION

"In the beginning was the Word, and the Word was with God, and the Word was God." — John 1:1

I would like to share with you some words from my Father, given to me along my walk and journey of life. They helped change my life and my walk. I pray they will be a blessing to you on your Christian journey.

My prayer is you to seek His Words and to walk with your hands in His. As His child, in your beginning, you have to know His Word. Why? Because in the beginning was the Word. That is where it all starts, in our beginnings—when we first start hearing words. Whose voices do we listen to, and whose words do we believe?

In sharing these words, I am sharing my life, my testimony, and my love for Jesus. Most of all, I am sharing God's Word. We all are on a journey to find something or someone. Jesus wants to be that someone. Listen to His Word and follow His path. His path will lead you all the way from earth to heaven.

Once you find out how loved you are by God our Father, your life will change. Mine did. My walk changed, literally and figuratively. The way that I used to walk was not pleasing to my new lover, Lord, and Savior, Jesus Christ. I changed my walk to please Him and to make Him proud of me. He made me special and set me aside from the world. I want to wear my lover's label to show the world that I belong to Jesus Christ, the lover of my soul.

Words from My Father is a collection of writings inspired by God, my Father. There are poems, parts of my story, and most importantly, my sermon notes from my pastor, Tracy E. Ventus, of New Mission Missionary Baptist Church in Cincinnati, OH. The message is the same in every line, word, and thought. God loves us so very much—so very, very much. Please let these "Words from My Father" plant a seed in your spirit that will bear much fruit.

I pray God bless and keep you in His Perfect will.

With much love,

Arethia

WALKING
IN THE BEGINNING

"And thine ears shall hear a word behind thee, saying, this is the way, walk ye in it, when ye turn to the right hand, and when ye turn to the left." — Isaiah 30:21

once knew a woman whose desperate search took her to bars six nights a week, searching for love; but on Sundays she sat at home and cried because she was so empty and had no one to love her. Her satisfaction came from sex, drugs, and alcohol. Then one Sunday, she chose a new lover, Jesus Christ, the lover of her soul, and dear God, did she change!

I was that woman.

DAY 1

ords have always been very important to me. I grew up an abused child. Not physically, but verbally. My father hated me. I am the middle child of three children, all four years apart. I had one older brother and have a younger sister, but for some reason, my father hated me. I was the one he would spew his ugly and cold words on. I can remember how my father would sit outside my bedroom door, at the top of the stairs, and tell me how horrible I was, how he could not wait to throw dirt on my grave. I was only about eight or nine years old.

Those became my words . . . my words from my father.

Writing became my way of escaping his cruel words. I began to write him hate letters. I poured my young tender heart into those letters, telling him how much he was hurting me for no reason I could see. I was obedient, received straight A's as a student, and did everything to please him, but he still hated me. I never missed Sunday school; I had to be there because my father was a deacon! I was shy and very withdrawn.

I would write and write and then tear the letters up into little pieces, so he would not find them and use more cold, cruel words to hurt me. English was my passion in school, and I loved to read. I discovered that words could heal, make me smile, and take me places my eyes never would or could see.

I began to write short stories and love poems. There was an inner voice that told me what words to write. It seemed that the deeper in despair I was, the more words were poured into me to write.

Words . . . beautiful words

The Gift

The beauty of the day is before me,

like a present waiting to be opened.

What does it hold inside, what's in the box?

I peep in a little at a time.

Why, I think it is wonderful,

this gift I've just received!

Now, let's see what I will do with my gift.

The Equipping of the Saints

Ephesians 4:4

To be equipped is to have the tools to do what we have been called to do. God wants us to be properly equipped to fight. He provides us with everything we need to go through the pressures of life. We have to know how to stand and be holy. With God, we can become what He planned and purposed for our lives. It starts with the renewing of our mind.

God renewed my mind as I wrote the words He gave me. Early on, even before I knew Him well, He equipped me with the tools I needed to do what I was called to do.

QUESTIONS TO PONDER:

What does this Scripture mean to you?

What tools do you need to fight the good fight of faith?

DAY 2

The love that I have for my family is very strong. The journey that my brother, sister, and I traveled was a rough one—some events happening by choice, some by chance. But we did not travel it alone. My mother's love and her prayers, I believe and know, were heard by God. It was only His grace and mercy that gave us His protection as we journeyed through our lives.

Father

Father, Father, I reach my hand to Thee;

no other help do I see.

Show me Your mercy.

Your strength I do so need.

I feel weary and worn

by life's cares and woes;

no other source of help do I plead.

Hear my cries in the darkened night.

Hear my sobs in the morning light.

Ease my pain and still my fears.

I place my hand,

my heart, and my soul in Your care.

Guide me, show me the splendor of Your might.

Show me, Father,

show me Your love, Your light.

Your child,

Your child is afraid of the dark.

Tell me, dear Father, tell me

it will soon be all right.

God Wants Us to Be a Blessing

II Timothy 1:6

The pit in my life made me realize whom I served. Weeping may endure for a night (or season), but joy comes in the morning light, in season! I had to go through something to get somewhere. God always has the last move.

QUESTIONS TO PONDER:

What does this Scripture mean to you?

Have you ever been in a pit? How did you arrive at your morning light?

DAY 3

The enemy had encased me in his wrapping, and I believed everything he said about who I was, but in time I would discover whose I was, and that has made all the difference in my life!

I've Been Told

A strong black woman,

I've been told,

is often much alone.

She wears her strength like a cape

surrounding her pain and fears.

So no one knows for sure

how really weak she is. . . .

It's only when she's alone

that the cape will slowly drop

and then reveal the thing she holds so dear.

That is the mask

she wears so well

to hold back all of her tears.

The Woman at the Well

John 4:13-18

The woman at the well was very much like me, searching for something (love), but each time I thought love had come, it failed and fell apart.

This woman was carrying her bucket, like many of us do. We are all carrying some kind of bucket looking to have it filled. God asks us to give Him our bucket, so He can fill it and bless us. Satan was trying to destroy her, but thank God, she ran in to Jesus.

When you have Jesus, you have it all. Some of us have to go through something to get to Him. When we come to Jesus, we have to surrender all and let go of our bucket.

QUESTIONS TO PONDER:

What does this Scripture mean to you?

How can God fill your bucket so that you are blessed?

DAY 4

Over the years I became a young unwed mother of three, searching so desperately for love. I carried so much sadness and had left behind so many failed relationships, but I still had my words.

Only God and His awesome, wonderful, caring love can turn mean, cold words into expressions of joy, peace, and love.

.

Merry-Go-Round

Here I go. Here I go again.

Falling in love, falling out of love. Fall down. Get up.

Start over again.

But I'm so tired of "here I go again." Please, can't this merry-go-round

slow down.

Here I go, here I go again. We met. We talk. We laugh.

We fall in love.

"You are so sweet."

You hear that and say that, over and over again.

Then the fall from grace. A word, a thought, an action.

It's no matter what starts the pain.

Here I go again; here I go again.

Now I have to forget you,

release you and myself to love again, and again

and again.

Here I go again. Here I go again. Here I go. Again.

Fountain of Living Water

Jeremiah 2: 9-13

Sin came when I tried to find pleasure outside of God's will. I looked for something else to make me satisfied. The closer I was getting to God, the more fulfilled my life became. God wanted me to get totally in the fountain of His living waters. I had to get totally deep in my relationship with God. God is the source of life. My God is able to do it all.

QUESTIONS TO PONDER:

What does this Scripture mean to you?

Have you ever been in the fountain of living water? How did it feel?

DAY 5

I hated my job and was also in a dead-end relationship. My sister had health issues at the same time my brother had mental issues. I was searching for so much, but I was holding onto the seed that was planted in me as a child. I was so alone, hurting so badly, but I was holding onto my faith that a change would come.

Alone

This message is for all the people

who think they stand alone.

If you are a single mother or father,

old and no one cares for you . . . anymore,

physically or mentally disabled,

your wife or husband no longer loves you . . . .

There is never anyone there to care for you . . .

or so it seems . . . .

But when you think you stand alone, that is when God,

our Father, is giving you special time with Him.

Now it is just you and Him.

Now He will let you lay your head in His lap,

put your hand on His knee, and listen to Him talk just to you.

He will say,

My precious little one, tell Me where it hurts.

"Oh Daddy, I feel so betrayed." I know my child.

"I feel so stabbed in my heart." I know my child.

"I feel so put down." I was also, my precious one.

Then He will wipe your tears away,

lift up your head and say,

The world did the same thing to my Son,

but He rose, and so can you.

My sweet baby, My child, you can rise also.

You and I are together.

I am in you and you are in My care.

We are in union with each other,

and you will never be alone as long as I have you.

Never, ever will you be alone.

I, and I alone will be with you.

Trust Me to the end.

The Gift of Compassion

Romans 12:13, 2 Corinthians 7:3

The comfort of Jesus cannot be replaced with anything or anyone. Jesus sent the Comforter to us when He left this earth. He did not leave us comfortless. The compassion Jesus shows me is because He knows what I am going through at all times. There is no trial that I have that is unknown to Him.

No matter what I was going through, Jesus saw me through. He had His hand outstretched to pull me closer to

Him and into the safety of His arms. No matter how bad it seemed, God had comfort just for me.

Comfort others with God's love. He will keep you in your storm to be a blessing to others in their storms. You have a testimony because you passed the test.

QUESTIONS TO PONDER:

What do these Scriptures mean to you?

How have you shown compassion to others when they were in a storm?

DAY 6

"But she that liveth in pleasure is dead while she liveth."

— I Timothy 5:6

"Search" is a verb, an action word. It means "to go through carefully and thoroughly in an effort to find something (Webster's Dictionary)." Other words to describe search are: to pursue, undertake, engage in, take in hand, endeavor, chase, run after, to shape one's course, to follow.

I was searching. I was in very active pursuit of *something*. Right or wrong, good or bad, I was using my time, energy, effort, money, heart, health, and soul in my search. That search took me places that only God's grace and mercy could cover me in. That search left me so thirsty, dwelling in dry, parched, foreign places.

Searching

I'm looking for love . . . .

Where are you looking?

Why, in all the right places!

I go to "Slides" every Friday night,

shake my butt, wearing my dress real tight.

Where are you looking?

On Saturday night, I date and mate my find

from shaking my behind.

Where are you looking?

Over to "Joe's" on Wednesday.

The wings are hot and the guys all drool

as I sit at the bar, smoking a Kool.

Where are you looking?

Thursday, got to go to "Latts."

The men come in looking sharp and smooth,

waiting for me to make my move.

Sashay to the ladies' room real nice and slow,

so they can see I've got more than any woman they could ever hope to know.

Where are you looking?"

On Monday there is a spot where all the fella's hang.

Why, there are three men for every woman,

and you know that's a lot.

If you can't get a man from that bunch

then honey, take off the spandex and hang up the pumps.

Oh, I forgot, Ladies Night on Tuesday at "Crazy Lucy's."

You can drink all night for free.

Just be careful. Don't wrap your car around no tree.

Where do you go on Sunday?

What a dumb question to ask.

There is no place to go on Sunday.

That's the day I sit alone and cry,

and wonder why,

why, dear God, why

won't you send me a guy?

Only He Satisfies My Soul

Psalm 63:5, Psalm 107:9

I thought my decisions were mine alone and that I could bear the consequences of them. The enemy wanted me to think that whatever I wanted, I should have, that whatever I wanted to do, I should do. The world tells us that we deserve to have the "good life." Never mind that the "good life" can be sending our bodies to an early grave and our souls to hell. My poem, "Searching," is evidence that I was searching for the answer to my pain in a man. I was looking for my will to be done.

QUESTIONS TO PONDER:

What do these Scriptures mean to you?

What does your soul truly long for?

DAY 7

"As the deer pants for the water brooks, so pants my soul for You, O God. My soul thirsts for God, for the living God." — Psalms 42:1-2

My life's journey was mapped according to what I searched after. My walk, my search for fulfillment was what my soul "panted" after—it desired and was breathless for the thing I needed to exist.

Keep Trying

Alone is so sad a word.

I sometimes feel that way.

To wish for someone

to hold and love and kiss my cares away—

is it really too much to ask?

I guess so . . . .

So here I sit, with pen and paper,

but not a mate in sight!

But by whose hand is that

I often ask myself.

For there were many who tried to share my time,

this time I spend alone,

but I beat them back

and then sit and cry,

"Oh my, oh my . . .

I really . . . did really . . . try."

He Will Never Leave You

Hebrews13:5, Deuteronomy 31:6

The enemy wanted to steal, kill, and destroy my life. God wanted to add joy, peace, and happiness to it. The enemy wanted to subtract all those blessings and fill my life with sadness, doubt, and confusion. He is the father of lies. He lives in confusion. That is why I was so miserable—I wasn't worshiping in Spirit and in truth.

Today there is freedom is walking with my Lord and Savior, Jesus Christ—the freedom to pursue the purpose He has in my life. God has a purpose for my life and yours. He was with me when I felt completely alone; He wanted to be the one I reached out for to fill my soul. And I finally saw Him there and reached back. I'm finally whole, and He will never leave me, ever.

QUESTIONS TO PONDER:

What do these Scriptures mean to you?

Do you believe that God will never leave you, that He never did? Does your life reflect that?

DAY 8

ittle did I know it, but God was preparing me and purging me. When I wrote the poem "Searching," it took me a long time to read it to someone. You see, that poem held very strong meanings and messages. It was very personal to me. It was completed in a time I was in my "purge season," my searching season. I was living in my own choice of "pleasure" and was dead inside.

A Love Letter

[A BIRTHDAY PRESENT FROM MY DADDY]

Hello, my child, I greet you in love. From the one who loves you best,

when you thought no one could ever love you.

Then you found that one true love light at the end of that long and dark tunnel.

That tunnel that twists and turns with all you go through

"looking for love."

That tunnel that has a small beam of light

that you hold onto with a strength that

I give you from within . . . .

Within where? you ask. Within your soul—

that spot that screams!

Hold on, hold on . . . I'm coming to rescue you!

My baby, my child; I will always supply your escape.

You need never fear, because I am with you always.

I will never leave you nor forsake you.

Your tears that you cry now will be wiped away.

Joy, peace, and love will flood your heart.

All of your tears will be wiped away.

Your mother's tears

were wiped away, and so will yours.

Don't fear, because my children need never fear.

You are mine. I know you

and I love you and always will.

Trust in Me to take you through.

Happy Birthday, from your Daddy, with love.

(Inspired on my birthday, July 30)

Entering into His Rest

Matthew 4:23-24

You do not have to be burdened down when you have Jesus. You can count on Him. We all are looking for love, but Jesus is the only perfect love.

QUESTIONS TO PONDER:

What does this Scripture mean to you?

When have you needed rest, and what did you do to get it?

DAY 9

MY journey through poetry showed my longing and search for the faith I now have in my Lord and Savior Jesus Christ. Alone, sad, and confused, I still sought God's Words. The Words from my Father all flowed with the same message; how much He loves me.

Poems and short stories were given to me when I was searching for and longing for love. Even though I didn't know Jesus was loving me so very much, He was pouring His words into my very being to be used for His glory and my salvation. I wrote about the hurt, the pain, the praise, the trials, the triumphs; and through it all, I remembered that He loves me and He cares, and He will never put more on me *than I can bear.*

Let Go and Let God

Never hold real tight

to things you think you could not bear to lose.

Never clutch them to your bosom,

close to your heart,

and swear by your god, the moon,

and all the above, that to part with this would

wound your soul;

for God will snatch them away from you

in a blink of an eye.

Never things, people, places, all so vain.

It can rip, slip, and be gone away,

of no value to anyone but you . . . .

They cast lots for Jesus's robe!

What a mockery your babbles will make

to cold-hearted people

who did not love you anyway.

But our Father has a plan, within the plan, within the plan,

and so on and so on.

That will have to be for others to see. And see they will, for light has no fellowship with darkness.

Things, they come into our possession and then you die . . .

and now someone else is the new owner.

Things have no loyalty to anyone.

Anyone can own a thing, but God our Father doesn't give things.

He gives good and perfect gifts. You don't have to buy it,

lease it, or put it in layaway.

It's free! No strings attached.

You cannot earn it. He just gives it.

That's what you hold close to your heart.

The good and perfect gifts from your Father

given at your start.

His gift of love for

someone like me

is so awesome,

so awesome to see.

Rapture in His Love

John 13:13

When God's love touches you, you cannot stay the same. It does not matter what you go through when God loves you, you are complete in Him. God loves you as much as He loves Jesus. He loves us because it is His choice. Choose to love Him back.

QUESTIONS TO PONDER:

What does this Scripture mean to you?

What does it feel like to be touched by God's love?

DAY 10

began to go back to church. I would listen, really listen to the message God was giving His messenger. I started writing what I heard as it flowed from Him to me. Through the words my Father gave to my pastor, Pastor Tracy Ventus, I found my Father's love and the gift He gave me—His words!

The Spirit kept giving me more words to write—words to seed into people's lives and to uplift them and let them know how much God loved them and would always be there for them. God's gift of words saved my life and saved my soul. To use His words to encourage those on their journeys, and to find God's love and their gifts, is a blessing to them and me. When I am in the house of the Lord, I try to write what the man of God is saying to *me*. I get into a zone and have no clue what I am writing.

The Door

Faith unlocks any door that has been shut

closed, and tightly sealed.

The door you shut on yourself is

the one hardest to open.

It is the one hardest to allow God's grace to open.

But it's only when God is allowed to open the door

for you and with that you realize that

with Faith in Him, all things are possible.

And when you open that door,

know that your Father has your hand in His.

He will lead you across the threshold into a

new and glorious beginning.

What you feared was beyond the door,

You should not have feared at all,

so swing the door open wide.

Fling it open and rejoice,

for my Father told me

I can do all things through Christ

who strengthens me.

Thank you, Jesus, for getting the door (see Philippians 4:13).

Lord Make Me a Blessing

Ephesians 4:11

If God can pull me out of sin and bondage, I should be able to help others as they struggle in this world. God puts a seed in us to be a blessing to others. Satan is trying to get us under his influence and so is God. We have to yield to the power of God and do His will. We have to be a blessing in order to receive a blessing. (You have to protect what comes in your spirit and what goes out.)

QUESTIONS TO PONDER:

What does this Scripture mean to you?

Who have you blessed today?

DAY 11

These nuggets were speaking to my spirit. There were times that I would go back days, weeks, and years later and remember what was going on in my life at the time of the sermon. These messages told me, "Hold on just a little bit longer. God loves you, and He will make a way out of no way."

Ask

Ask, only of your Father

To Him alone cry out.

Do not turn your head

from side to side to man.

Do not go.

But look up,

look to the heavens.

There your answer will flow.

Ask only of your Father.

This I truly know—

His children, their cry He hears.

Before the tear glistens in your eye,

His plan for that tear was formed long ago.

His beam of light is steady,

just look to Him alone,

just ask of your Father;

He wants to give you a throne.

The Lord Gives Us the Things We Need

Matthew 6:11, Psalms 104:26

God wanted me to know that He supplies all of my needs. We all have needs that we try to fill on our own. I had to wait on Him to supply my needs in due season.

QUESTIONS TO PONDER:

What do these Scriptures mean to you?

What do you need right now?

DAY 12

was so messed up at one time, I wanted to end my life. I would have erased all the awesome plans God has for my life. God's Word stepped into my life from the sermon notes, my poems, plays, and short stories. I began to see there is beauty in ashes. I began to read His Word. I learned how much God loves me. He gave His Son, Jesus Christ, to show how much He loves me. His Words tell me over and over about His love for me.

The Twins

Grace and mercy pours down on me

like drops of rain on my thirsty soul.

For I was dead in my trespasses and sin

but . . . your grace and mercy stepped right in.

Thank you, Jesus, thank you, Lord

for loving me when I couldn't find a friend.

When I didn't know You and had no hope,

grace and mercy extended my rope,

letting me know Your Word is true.

Turn to the Master; He will see you through—

through the pain, through the tears, your fears,

your disappointments, your shame.

Trust in Jesus; there is power in His name.

When you call on the Master,

He'll send His twins.

Grace and Mercy will rush right in!

His Purchased Passion

Mark 10:17, Luke 7:36

I promised God I would go where He told me to go, say what He wanted me to speak. I wanted to do His will, not mine. He took my ashes and gave me beauty. He took my confusion and gave me peace. I had to trust God in all areas of my life. His appointed end for me is good. God is in control of my life, even in the storms. He will always make a way out of no way.

I chose to trust Him. God is always in the process of healing me. He will never leave me nor forsake me. I cannot trust in riches, only in God can I trust. When I don't know where my life is going is when He wants me to walk by faith, not by sight.

QUESTIONS TO PONDER:

What do these Scriptures mean to you?

Who or what is in control of your life right now?

DAY 13

"Love not the world, neither the things that are in the world. If any man love the world, the love of the Father is not in Him. For all that is in the world, the lust of the flesh, and the lust of the eyes, and the pride of life, is not of the Father, but is of the world. And the world passeth away, and the lust thereof; but he that does the will of God abideth forever." — 1 John 2:15-17

As my walk started changing, the places and things I used to do changed also. My search changed from outside of me to inside of me.

When I turned my search for fulfillment away from the world and the desires of the flesh to the only lasting love and fulfillment, Jesus Christ, then my search was over and now I know who to listen to and follow.

Messing with Me

How can I let somebody

who is messed up himself

mess me up?

When one blind person falls into a ditch,

he will pull another blind person in with him

(if they are connected together),

'cause they both are blind, and everybody knows

the blind cannot lead the blind.

So . . .

if you have messes in your head and heart,

that means you might mess me up,

and if I follow someone just like you into a ditch,

I'll also go.

But thank God, somebody like me has a daddy like you, my Father.

Even when I let my head, heart, body, and soul get messed up,

You come along and snatch me back into Your fold

(and disconnect me from what I should have not been connected to anyway).

Daddy, I fell into a ditch time after time.

But time after time, when I was in that ditch,

You pulled me out

and gently set me back on solid ground.

Go Tell, I've Been Changed

II Corinthians 5:17

I wanted my walk to match with my talk. God made me a new creature from His Words. Every new situation gives me the opportunity to act out of my Christianity. I have to be in a continuous process of changing, getting closer to God, and acting more like Jesus. To hear the Word and to be a doer of the Word creates my change. When I understand God's revelation, it turns into an illumination.

QUESTIONS TO PONDER:

What does this Scripture mean to you?

How has God made a change in your walk?

DAY 14

developed a love relationship with my heavenly Father. I now have a Father who loves me. I found my heavenly Father and His Son, Jesus Christ. I found a spiritual father too—Pastor Tracy Ventus is my pastor, my mentor, my shepherd, and was my spiritual covering when I was single.

My pastor's words spoke to the brokenness of my relationship with my earthly father and my heavenly Father. My earthly father hated me, but I had no idea how much my heavenly Father loved me. No matter what method I used to seek out love, it failed until I found Jesus Christ. Only then did I find what I was searching for. Only then was I filled with true love.

Lord, Help Me to Stand

Lord, help me to stand and do Your will.

Your love I want to always feel.

I've hurt You and disappointed You so much in my life.

Because of this, I've had my share of strife,

But Your grace and mercy stepped right in

each time I fell back into sin.

Please, sweet Jesus, help me to be strong.

Give me the strength to sing a new song.

Be my sword, my bulwark, and my shield.

Help me, sweet Jesus, to do Your will.

In You I have hope, in You I have life.

This, dear God, I know is right.

My flesh is nothing, nothing can it gain.

My feelings are tools Satan tries to claim.

He wants my soul and my body too.

I scream in the night and cry in the day.

Dear God, my God, please help me to stand

locked in Your love, strong in Your might,

knowing and trusting it will soon be alright.

Oh How Great is Thy Faithfulness

Galatians 5:22

In the name of Jesus, I can rebuke Satan and make him move out of my way. God gives more goodness and mercy through His faithfulness. God will fulfill His Word if I just stand. He will be faithful to me. I do my part and God will do His part. God will do exactly what He said He would do.

QUESTIONS TO PONDER:

What does this Scripture mean to you?

In what ways this week have you been faithful?

DAY 15

Pastor Ventus's sermons have been a light that was sent to shine in the dark places of my life. His words from God spoke to the brokenness in my life. His sermons were given to him to lead me back into relationship with God and my Savior, Jesus Christ. It is then that true worship took place.

The love my Father has for a nasty, horrible, sinner like me is beyond awesome. The plans He has for my life with Him were beyond my understanding. I want to share God's gift of His Words. These words helped me understand His words and His love for me. I had to have a relationship with my Father to live the life He wants for me. He wants His children to soar!

Ships - Get on Board

Ships.

Friendship, the one we get on first.

It's such a delight, this new and wonderful ship.

So many pleasant little and big surprises.

Oh me, oh my, I like this friendship.

Relationship

The next vessel we board. Oh the joys of first getting on.

Your every wish is the ship captain's sole job to command.

The commitment of the relationship.

But what happens when quite by accident

we get on the "battleship?"

I thought you said right, not left!

How on earth did we get on a new ship?

Flee, flee, let's abandon this sinking ship.

Please, help, dear God. Help! Find us another ship!

Lo . . . look there in the distance . . . .

I think I see a different kind of ship.

Hurry, let's get on board.

Now I feel good, don't you? Get comfy,

get settled, let's set sail.

With this ship we can go far. The name of this ship,

the one we all need,

Companionship.

God is Calling His Children to Soar:

In Training to Fly like an Eagle

Proverbs 22:6

God does not want me to flap my wings on the ground, but to soar in the sky. I wanted to train my children to soar, to train them in God's way. I had to soar, to show them how. God had called me to soar, and I had to submit to His will for my life. That sounds so simple and easy: "Submit to His will," but that is the hardest part of this walk. To let go of self-dependency, self-reliance, and self-importance (ego) was impossible on my own. I had to say to God daily, "Thy will be done, on earth (we are made from dirt-earth) as it is in heaven" (Matthew 6:10).

To achieve the greatness that was planted in me before my creation, Jesus had to be the potter and I had to be the clay. To fulfill that longing, that burning for my vision, I had to submit. It was no longer about what I could do on my own, but what God could do through me to give Him glory. To walk in love into His kingdom is a holy walk.

What God wants for you and your children is their greatness to be achieved and His purpose made evident.

.

QUESTIONS TO PONDER:

What does this Scripture mean to you?

What will it take to make you soar?

DAY 16

was always the caregiver in my family. I cared for my mother, who was my shining star. She was always saying, "I am so proud of you." Her proudest moment was to see me graduate from college. It was also the proudest moment for me and my three children. Despite suffering from cancer and being in pain, she attended my graduation.

She died a year later. Her one request was for me to take care of my sister and brother. I tried to do my best to honor that request. I thought it was an honor, not a burden.

Burdens

When I care for others

You care for me.

When I bear others' burdens,

You bear mine.

Serving others

is serving You.

"In as much as you did it for the least of my brethren,

You did it unto Me."

The Divine Calling of Parenthood

Deuteronomy 11:2

God was and is watching over my entire life and the lives of my children and loved ones. If I do what He says to do, He will bless me. I have the Holy Spirit to fight my battles, if I stay in position. My faith helps to keep me in position to stand. I need to stand on God's Word and principles for my children and relatives.

QUESTIONS TO PONDER:

What does this Scripture mean to you?

What position do you have in your family or with your relatives?

DAY 17

y pastor promised on my wedding day he would cover my husband and me. I love my spiritual father so much. I give to you these words from my Father as they were given to me—with love, to help you on your journey to find what we all crave and need to be fulfilled. The love of Jesus will carry you on your search for Him, just as He did on mine.

Words are the way to understand each other, but most importantly, to understand God. He gives freely of Himself to us through His words. We have to study His Word to know His heart. When you know His heart, it will be easy to let Him in. He will become your Lord and Savior and the lover of your soul. His Words of love will cover you for life. Words are such powerful things. They can be used to kill or bring forth life. God's Words are life to you, a lamp to your feet. I thank Him for sending His Words to me. They are a soothing balm.

The Soothing Balm

Peace of mind,

the soothing balm

that comes like a whisper in your ear,

breathing life into you

and chasing away

all the darkness and fears

that try to steal your joy.

If anything tries to steal it,

fight;

fight long and hard to reclaim it.

Your Father, the King

gave us, His children, that joy

because He loves us so much.

He's that soothing balm, whispering in your ear,

saying to you,

"Be still, my child, and let Me breathe life into you,

And then you will be ready to

accept all my gifts.

My gift of peace, My gift of joy,

and my greatest gift of all,

My love for you."

[Inspired by my granddaughter, Danielle.]

The Ministry of Ambassadors

II Corinthians 5:20

There is a reason for God changing me. There is purpose in my life. There is purpose in your life. God has put us in a position to give Him glory. He is the God of our past, present, and future. We really do not know all that God has put inside of us, but it's possibly the power to turn the world around.

We cannot judge others or ourselves according to the flesh. Only God knows our true selves; He knows what He has invested in each of us. God plants seeds in us to grow into a mighty tree for Him. Grow your seed.

QUESTIONS TO PONDER:

What does this Scripture mean to you?

How can you grow the seed God has planted in your life?

DAY 18

All of my poems are extensions of my life. They come to guide me, show me, and most of all teach me. The poem I wrote, "Searching," wanted to be expanded and grow. The poem took on a life of its own, with characters, a plot, and most of all, a message.

The poem grew as I grew in God's grace and mercy and His Word, and it grew from a poem to a three-act play. What did God do? During one of the most depressed times of my life, the nineties, He helped me write my first play, *Come Sunday*. The road from the poem's beginning to the play's opening night was all God's work.

People gave their time, talent, and money to make it happen. *Come Sunday* created the playwright in me and helped change not only my life, but thousands of other lives. The words were used in a mighty way; people were saved and their lives were given to Christ.

A Message

Guide me, Father.

Show me.

Teach me.

I want to grow in Your grace and mercy.

I want to grow in Your Word.

My life has a message

because of Your work in me,

and the more You work in me,

the more of a life-giver I become.

Pray in the Will of God

1 John 5:14

My prayer life had to be in the will of God, my Father. There is power in praying in the will of God. It is so powerful that the enemy wanted to steal it from me. He did not want me to pray to my Father for anything. He wanted me to believe that I could do things on my own. I had trained myself to believe my life was in my own hands, that I was the master of my fate, captain of my ship.

If my prayer life has no substance, there can be very little God can do for me or with me. My prayer life is my connection to God.

QUESTIONS TO PONDER:

What does this Scripture mean to you?

Are your prayers in the will of God?

DAY 19

In the play *Come Sunday* there are two main characters. One is a praying sister—the example of how we are accountable for our sisters and brothers. She's the older sister, the caregiver, and she wants to see her sister saved. The other is a younger sister that only wants to drink, party, and "enjoy" her life.

The play revolves around the two sisters and how God allows turnaround in our lives at all times. The two sisters are completely different, but God's love binds them together. Their roles are explored in the play in an explosive way.

What does God say about how we are to treat our sisters and brothers? That should be our standard, but it's not.

Love

Father,

You have put so many people in my life

for a reason and a season.

They are all so different,

but Your love binds us together.

Your love in me

binds us together.

Help me to love them and treat them

with the same love you have for me.

And He Has Given Us This Command

1 John 4:21, Philippians 2:2

You have to *choose* to walk in love. *You have to choose* to walk in this new direction. Walking in love with Jesus Christ your Lord, your lover, your Savior beside you, and His Spirit inside of you, is a *choice.*

I did not know that Jesus wanted to be my lover. He was just waiting for me to choose Him to love me. I had no idea what walking in love was. I did not know that the Lord would supply my every need (see Philippians 4:19) because He loves me so very much.

Jesus will carry all your burdens, trials, and tribulations. He is able and willing to help—all you have to do is trust in Him and *ask,* and it shall be done (see John 15:7). I asked Him to help me stand, and with His help, I was able to stand.

QUESTIONS TO PONDER:

What do these Scriptures mean to you?

Who can you ask God to help you love? How can you treat your brothers and sisters better?

DAY 20

My sister had health issues at the same time my brother had mental issues. I was searching for so much when I wrote my play, *Come Sunday*, for myself and for my family. But God showed me how He heard my prayers. Just like He heard my mother's prayers, He heard and answered mine also—in His time, His way and His will, not mine. This is shown over and over in the play in each character's life. The play shows that there are burdens that we bear for our families that are unique to all families, but God hears our unique prayers and knows what we can bear. The sisters learn it's all about God's plan for their lives and what He has seeded into them. The waiting for the results of their prayers is a test for their testimony; that is what our hope is built on. Our hope is in Jesus Christ and His Word!

Father

God, You heard my prayers

and answered me

in your time,

Your way, Your will,

not mine.

My hope is in You, Lord.

I choose to trust that Your plan

is the best one for me.

I'm working up a great testimony.

Oh Ye of Little Faith

Matthew 8:26

The key, the secret golden nugget God gave me is so crucial, so important, I cling to it daily. If I had missed this, or not understood this, I could never have begun this awesome journey. The secret? *This walk is not for every Christian.*

WHO IS IT NOT FOR? It is not for the Christian with little faith in the abundance of God's love (see Ephesians 3:17-19). It is not for the Christian with little faith that God will supply your every need (see Psalms 23:1). It is not for the Christian with little faith in God's promises (see II Peter 3:9). It's not for Christians with little faith, period.

WHO IS THE WALK FOR? It is only for the Christian who is willing to trust God (see Proverbs 3:5,6). It is only for those who are ready to "mount up with wings as eagles; they shall run and not be weary; and they shall walk, and not faint" (Isaiah 40:31).

I had to go through the wilderness to get to the promised land that the building (my vision) was planted on. To go through the wilderness, I had to have my lover (Jesus) with me. I couldn't leave home without Him. He pointed me in the right direction and equipped me with the faith to move from one spot in this journey to the next. And He can do the same for you.

QUESTIONS TO PONDER:

What does this Scripture mean to you?

Where can you plant your mustard seed of faith so it can grow?

DAY 21

"I wait for the Lord, my soul doth wait, and in His word do I hope."
— Psalms 130:5

saw myself as both characters in the play, as the two sisters, Camille and Jamella. I was the older sister that was trying to bring her baby sister back to the Lord, and I was the baby sister who was looking for love in dark and empty places, people, and things.

Come Sunday shows how we can be a leader and a follower at the same time. Leading people that we love to Christ by being a follower is the very best example, but are we worthy to be a leader? What does the leader's walk look like?

The older sister goes to church each and every Sunday and calls her baby sister to come join her, but every Sunday she refuses to come to church. Believing her baby sister will never change, that she will never see the results of her praying, she begins to be discouraged. Depression and discouragement sets in when she feels no hope. But thank God, Jesus is our hope. The play shows that waiting on the Lord is where our hope lies. Depending on His Word is where we have to stand.

Waiting

I'm waiting on You, Lord . . . .

Your Words give me hope.

Whether afraid, alone, discouraged, or depressed,

lost, afraid at the end of my rope,

my hope, my help, my everything

is in you, Lord.

Trust in God, Depend on His Word

Proverbs 3:5

When we think a situation will never change, that God will never answer our prayers—even if we ask, and pray, and cry, and it still will not change—is when God will do a *Come Sunday* in our lives, a turnaround. I learned how to trust in God completely, even when I was afraid and losing hope. The dragons/demons along the way? He slayed them for me, but I had to let Him. I had to trust Him.

God has prepared this path for you before the creation of the world. Jesus Christ, the lover of your soul, has everything you need to soar to take a leap of faith.

QUESTIONS TO PONDER:

What does this Scripture mean to you?

Are there demons or dragons you are willing to let Jesus slay?

DAY 22

think prayers sent to God for your sisters and brothers are special to God's ears. In the play, the older sister was constantly trying to get her sister to come to church, and little did she know that on Sunday, her clubbing baby sister sat alone in tears, wondering why God wouldn't send her what she thought was the answer—a guy. She was searching.

One sister rooted in how she was raised, the other straying away, thinking that she could find what she was searching for in clubs, people, and things. The play showed how the different characters, in the bars where she was a regular, were also searching.

That search for something /someone is played out as we follow 'Miss Lady," as she is called, for seven days, as she searches for what she already has—God's love.

No Wonder

Searching,

wanting,

crying out

for the things we think we need/want.

We have no idea what we really need/want.

It's no wonder we look for love in all the wrong places, and faces.

and even then, You're right there with us,

ready to share Your love, light and might!

Thank you, God, for seeing us through the darkest of night.

Drawn to Jesus

Jeremiah 31:3, Hosea 2:13-15

The nineties to me was the winter of a purging season. The "what of a what?" you say. You know—when God is purging you, trimming you, preparing you to walk in His glory. That winter was cold, dark, lonely, scary, and depressing. You know you are in a purging season when you throw a pity party and you're too depressed to come.

The hardest part of this walk is seeing this tall building far away in the distance (your vision) that is hazy and unclear, but it's beckoning you to come. You don't know why you feel this pull, this tug on your spirit; you just know you have to *move toward that place.*

QUESTIONS TO PONDER:

What do these Scriptures mean to you?

When you look back over your life, where can you see times Jesus was wooing you, pulling you closer to Him?

DAY 23

Another character that we meet in the hotspots Miss Lady frequents is Marcell, a married man who has a fling with her. He is a smooth-talking, coldhearted man, who is just out for some fun. She thought he would be the love of her life, not a one-night fling, but Marcell has problems of his own. He is searching for love too, but he's looking/lusting for it outside of his marriage. His search has a life-changing consequence he did not see coming.

Come Sunday shows how we take our vows and promises made to God too lightly, not caring about how we are hurting our Father, ourselves, and others with our disobedience. It shows that every action we take and choice we make has a consequence.

Consequences

In searching for what we think we want,

we are blind to the things other people around us need.

We don't see

how the pain we're in ourselves

affects everyone else.

Even the temporary things we find to fill that emptiness

never fill it.

They drain us,

killing our souls.

Every choice has a consequence attached,

good or bad.

Lord, lead me on the right path.

Never Satisfied

Micah 6:14

I suffered mentally, physically, and spiritually until I let go and let God take over my life. Until I became a follower of Christ and walked as He did, I suffered a break in my relationship with God, my Father. This break caused a feeling of aloneness and discontent that nothing was able to satisfy. No amount of drugs, sex, alcohol, food, money, material things, riches, or fame could satisfy me.

Nothing can refresh your soul but Jesus Christ. Your vision will never be revealed to you, nor your purpose made known to you, without your knowing the Father's heart and having Him come into yours.

QUESTIONS TO PONDER:

What does this Scripture mean to you?

How does God satisfy your soul?

DAY 24

The other supporting characters in the play also have hidden agendas—some good, some bad, some just as lonely as Miss Lady, desperately searching for fulfillment differently.

The play has a narrator, a bartender that keeps the humor coming as he dishes out about life and love in each night club. The people in *Come Sunday* begin to realize that God is a God of second chances in everyone's life, even theirs. The play offers hope to those who feel lost and alone. It shows that people everywhere are searching for something or someone, praying for something to fill them up. Only the love of Jesus can do that!

The end of the play has the audience crying and laughing at the same time. It teaches and entertains with a message that we all need to know. Prayers *do* work and people *do* change.

Minister Lyrica Joy, dancer in Come Sunday

Starting Over

Isaiah 43:19

I started forcing my feet to move in that direction (sometimes I wasn't sure which direction I was moving in), but my feet started moving. I took a step, then I took another and another. I still didn't know why I was being drawn, because Jesus had not revealed my purpose to me yet. I only knew I had become a follower of Jesus Christ.

I was now walking in a new direction, because I had become *new*. Old things (sinful actions and thoughts) had passed away. I had become a new creation because I was now abiding in Jesus Christ's love (see II Corinthians 5:7).

QUESTIONS TO PONDER:

What does this Scripture mean to you?

What new things has God been doing in your life lately?

DAY 25

" Come Sunday", premièred on December 26, 1997 to a sold-out crowd for three nights. It has been performed in theaters, schools, churches, nursing homes, prisons, and at private events. It has been performed for thousands.

My first play. Wow! I was so in awe as to how God could give me a poem, born out of my anguish and despair, and bless me through it with the gift of a hit play. Who knew? I did not, but God did. God gave me His words. They were more words from my Father.

God Leads

Walking worthy of my calling

is a battle,

but it is a battle that has already been won.

I must be in proper position.

A spring-cleaning is needed for this walk.

Lord, I am willing to get rid of all the old baggage

and garbage, to receive my blessings.

I submit to Your will for my life.

God Leads Us if We Let Him

Deuteronomy 32:12, Psalm 77:20

God put me in a place for a reason and a season—to make Himself Lord in my life. He shaped me and molded me to do His will, not mine. I was in my purging season because He was outfitting me for my walk.

If you are in His will, you are right where He wants you to be. There is a song that says "Let Jesus lead you. He will lead you all the way from earth to heaven." I believe that Jesus is a mighty good leader. Let Him lead you!

QUESTIONS TO PONDER:

What do these Scriptures mean to you?

How is God shaping you in this season of your life?

DAY 26

My play, *Come Sunday,* means more to me now than my poem. Sunday is the day I gather with family and friends and worship the awesomeness of God. Come Sunday means I can hear the Word of God through His chosen servant—words to heal, help, and restore my fellowship with my Father. The Word of God is what my soul "pants" for now.

Sunday is the day I hear sermons that connect God's Word to my life and teach me how to yield to His Spirit. The words that God gives His servants (pastors) speak to me on Sundays, and I write them down to remember "Your word is a lamp to my feet and a light to my path" (Psalms 119:105).

In your searching, be sure to remember to take your lamp; you will always need a light.

Your Word

Your Word tells me that with faith

anything is possible.

Your Word also tells me

it is impossible to please You without faith.

The world wanted me to believe

that the confidence and faith I had in myself

was what would give me peace, love, happiness, and success.

How foolish!

There is nothing I can do on my own strength.

The battle was never meant to be fought alone.

God's Word Gives Us Faith

I Timothy 6:12

God can only speak to my spirit. I have to be in the Spirit to talk to my Father. He will listen in the Spirit and answer in the Spirit. The flesh cannot talk to God. The Spirit is the connecting force. This force is so powerful that it can move mountains in our lives.

The battle is between the light of the world—our Lord and Savior, Jesus Christ—and the prince of darkness—Satan, our enemy. There is a fight for our soul. Jesus wants none to perish. The enemy wants to keep us in darkness and to keep us deceived by his lies. I repeat again, he wants to destroy us. Loving God's Word and using it in faith against Satan's lies will keep us strong.

QUESTIONS TO PONDER:

What does this Scripture mean to you?

What keeps you strong in your faith?

DAY 27

To begin this walk I had to first empty myself of what had been poured into me from the world's system of thinking and "think thoughts that are true, honest, just, pure, lovely, things of good report, and having virtue" (Philippians 4:8). I was told to feed my appetite, to appease the flesh, but the Word tells me that the flesh can profit nothing. I can see, feel, and touch the flesh, but the spirit was invisible to my eyes so I put little effort into its feeding. Walking by faith is so hard to do if my eyesight is turned outward and not inward.

Purity

I empty myself

before You.

Everything I had,

everything I have

I give to You.

Help me feed my soul well—

my soul, Father, and not my flesh.

Pour Your Word into me

so I can walk this walk full of only You.

We Become What We Focus On

Philippians 4:8

When I look into myself, I don't really see the awesome power God has instilled into my life. I see a miserable wretch hobbling in pain and confusion. But the beauty of being in Christ Jesus is being covered with His blood. He sees me as a born-again Christian who is saved by His grace and mercy.

He sees the woman who committed murder by aborting her babies as saved. He sees the man who committed adultery as saved. If sinners have confessed with their mouths and believed in their heart that Jesus is their Lord and Savior and asked for forgiveness of their sins, God is faithful to forgive them. Man is not.

QUESTIONS TO PONDER:

What does this Scripture mean to you?

What can you do to feed your spirit well?

DAY 28

Once God's Spirit was in me, there began to be evidence of it. When I accepted Jesus as my Lord and Savior, I wanted to change and be in His will. I have been called to do the work of my Father. I need to be about my Father's business.

There is a difference between religion and relationship. I had to be in relationship with Jesus in order to start this journey. This walk is not for the weak. I was walking into battle, the battle to gain my inheritance and to leap into my greatness. My strength has to come from my Lord, not from me. It is impossible to use my own strength. God is the only one who will fight for me until the end.

I Let You IN

Once I let You in,

Father,

Your Words,

The Words of my Father,

began to heal me from the inside out.

The more I know You

the more I love You,

the more open I am to Your loving strength;

and the more Your strength fills me,

the more whole I become.

Learning the Process of Discipleship

Luke 9:23, Romans 6:5

We all have a belief system. When we are in the process of becoming a Christian, we must change. We have to process that change. The cross that we carry is the cross of Jesus, and there is power in the cross. Our flesh was crucified on the cross, and we have the power to say no to sin. In Jesus there is more abundant life and joy.

QUESTIONS TO PONDER:

What do these Scriptures mean to you?

What are some of the areas in your life that you need/want power to change?

DAY 29

had to take off the "wrapping" the enemy had me in. To make this change, there was a tearing down and a ripping apart of what I had been told about *who* I was so I could realize *whose* I am—God's child. I was able to reconcile my feelings toward my father after my mother's death and let God be my healing balm. My father suffered from mental issues that I now understand as an adult. It helped to explain his feelings, words, and actions. It helped ease the hurt and the pain. It also helped me offer forgiveness, which I needed more than he did.

The truth about me was and is everything God (My Father) says about me—I was created in God's image, and that's something true and lovely (see Genesis 1:27).

I Am

I am Your beloved child,

and that's the truth.

You are my perfect Father,

and that's the truth too.

I know it now.

I know whose I am.

And that's enough for me.

Whose I Am

Proverbs 8:22

I was made at the beginning of God's creation, long before any of His plans of redemption went into effect. He created me to be a perfect reflection of Him, a precious child, a much-loved one. His redemption brings me back to that place of being His child. I am His and He is mine.

QUESTIONS TO PONDER:

What does this Scripture mean to you?

What does being fully God's and fully loved as His child mean to you?

DAY 30

My Father had to take off the old clothes I had on (the sinful urges of what the world said was right to do, say, and think) and put on my praise garments to supplement my faith. The moment I chose to walk in God's love, the journey began.

Forgiven

You are forgiven.

The moment you ask in your heart and confess with your mouth,

you are forgiven.

You are forgiven of all your sins.

Not just this day, this sin,

but of all your sins.

I paid the price for this room,

not the man that just left you.

I paid the price for your whole body.

I paid the price for your soul.

I paid the price way back on Calvary.

I paid with my blood.

By my stripes you are healed,

that you may have a right to the tree of eternal life.

I've been inside of you all this time.

Who do you think carried you all this time?

Me, the Spirit that lives inside your heart and soul;

the Spirit that brought you to this place of repentance.

I dwell inside you.

How much more intimate can anyone be?

My sweet child, I am what you are looking for.

I will never leave you, nor forsake you.

I am not fleeting.

I am not fickle and I am not unfaithful.

I will abide in you forever.

I am God.

I will love you forever, and forever, and forever,

until the end of time I will dwell inside you, forever!

Walking into a New Life with Jesus

II Pater 1:11

God is forgiving, man is not. Jesus can save the most sin-filled soul. All we have to do is let Him into our heart, our spirit, and let Him take over. Let Jesus lead you. If you put on these new garments (thoughts and actions), there will be richly provided for you an entrance into the eternal kingdom of our Lord and Savior Jesus Christ.

Jesus took care of everything for your trip a long time ago. He already paid the price. It was too much for you to pay. When He died on the cross, He prepared and prepaid the way for your walk of faith. He is willing and able to keep you from falling.

Are you ready? Did you choose Him as your companion on this journey? Do you feel the pull of greatness, the longing to run on and see what the end will be?

If you answered yes, yes, yes, turn your thoughts to God our Father and say:

"Dear God, my heavenly Father, I accept Jesus Christ as my Lord and Savior, the lover of my soul. I ask for and accept the forgiveness of my sins. I believe Your Word, my Father, that you will supply all my needs and you will never leave me nor forsake me. I submit to Your will for my life. I want to walk in love. I want to walk in Your love. Let the journey begin."

You have just established a covenant relationship with our Lord and Savior, Jesus Christ, and His blood now covers you. My fellow traveler, you are in for the journey of your life. You are now ready to leap into the arms of Jesus each time you get tired and weary. He will carry you from earth to heaven. The stops along the way are already planned—just listen to His instructions.

QUESTIONS TO PONDER:

What does this Scripture mean to you?

Your whole life is ahead of you. What would you like Jesus to do first in your life?

The Answer to All Our Questions

Jesus Christ,

our Lord and Savior

is the answer.

He is the author and finisher of our faith.

Read His book,

the Holy Bible,

a bestseller all over the world.

ACKNOWLEDGMENTS

All praise to God my Father for giving me a gift. God is so awesome. It's all about His Word.

I am so thankful He shared His Word with me. Jesus showed up and showed out in blessing me with this book, *Words from My Father*. The way it came together was God's doing, not mine. This was planned long before my creation. He put the right people in my life to make this a reality.

This book is dedicated to my brother, Norman Hornsby III. He was not only the most awesome brother God could have given me; he was my mentor, my advisor, and my first editor. He advised me on what to put in the book and listened very carefully to each selection. There are no words to express the loss of his presence in my life. He is now my angel. I know he is so pleased to see our hard work coming to fruition.

My family is my joy and my inspiration to do the very best that I can. My sister, Cleo Hornsby, is my sounding board and listens to my ideas and thoughts. I thank God for her. I thank God for my wonderful children—Ronald Kenneth Harris II, Jonathan Brian Hornsby, Shawnia Nicole Robertson, and all of my seed. God is truly blessing me. I am so proud of them all.

To my husband, Robert Rinfrow, my proofreader, a hit songwriter, and my rock: It is because of your belief in me that

I was able to produce this book. You gave me the support that only you could give. Thank you with all my love.

A special thank you to Dr. Cheri Westmoreland, who took a leap of faith with me and told me I could Soar. Without her push and encouragement, this would not have been anything but a collection of words. She helped me realize "with God all things are possible." I am so proud to say she is my editor.

To my pastor, mentor, and friend, Pastor Tracy E. Ventus, I can only say, "To God goes the glory." You have walked with me through my storms and through my peace. Because of your sermons, this book was birthed. You have been a blessing to me and my family, and we love you so very much.

I thank God my Father for gifting me with His words. Thank you to Jesus for being my one true love. Read His Word in the Holy Bible; they are a healing for your soul and a lamp unto your feet. I am so blessed to know Him, and so happy He knows me.

With much love,

Arethia Hornsby Rinfrow

ABOUT MY BIBLE STUDY NOTES

I give thanks to my pastor for giving me so many resources to pull from, for the portions of Bible study in each day's devotional. Most of the Bible study titles and Scriptures for each day were from notes I took during his Sunday sermons.

Reverend Tracy E. Ventus has been the pastor of New Mission Missionary Baptist Church since 1997. He is a compassionate and caring servant of God, who has a special place in his heart for senior citizens and children. His love and dedication to God and His people is felt in New Mission and throughout the Madisonville and Greater Cincinnati area.

Pastor Ventus loves the Lord. He believes in teaching and preaching the true gospel of Jesus Christ. He is a gifted preacher and teacher who makes the Word of God clear to all, no matter what their level of understanding may be.

He is well respected in the community as a true servant of God who believes in taking God outside the walls of the church and into the streets of the community. You may find Pastor Ventus walking the streets, shaking hands and holding conversations with the hurting, lost youth, the sick, discarded adults, and anyone else he is led to uplift.

His cool, quiet demeanor falls away when he steps up to the pulpit and lets the word of God come from his heart. His illustrative preaching style is captivating and touches the hearts, minds, and spirits of everyone who hears Him.

He is the husband of his beautiful wife, Portia, and the father of one son, Brittain. Pastor Ventus has a divinity bachelor degree at Cincinnati Christian University; now he will begin studying for his master's. The New Mission Church family is grateful for this anointed vessel of God.

ABOUT THE AUTHOR

Arethia Hornsby Rinfrow is a gifted writer and speaker who brings inspiring words into lives. With candor and humor, she shows God's love in her writings and workshops. As a woman of God, she has taken the struggles of her life and captured them in this first book, *Words from My Father,* which she hopes will deliver a message of inspiration and enjoyment to all who read it. She believes that everyone is gifted with a talent just waiting to be developed.

Arethia's passion is writing. She wrote a poem in 1993 that turned into her first play, *Come Sunday*, which premiered in 1997. It has been performed in theaters, schools, churches, and prisons. In total, she has written, produced, and directed eighteen plays.

Arethia is the founder/CEO of GFPT (Good Feet Production Troupe), a drama guild, founded in 1997. GFPT is a group of dedicated people using their God-given talents to spread a message of love, respect, and positive life choices through acting, singing, dancing, conferences, lectures, and seminars. GFPT will go anywhere there is a need to deliver this message. They are available to do workshops, seminars, and speaking engagements for organizations, churches, and private events.

Arethia Hornsby Rinfrow was born in Portsmouth, Virginia, to Norman and Elizabeth Hornsby. She was raised with two other siblings: a sister, Cleo, and a brother, Norman (who died in 2015). Arethia graduated from West Philadelphia High School and attended Bethune Cookman College for one year.

She joined New Mission Missionary Baptist Church under the current leadership of Pastor Tracy Ventus, many, many years ago. While raising her children, Arethia went back to college and received her baccalaureate degree from the University of Cincinnati in Psychology. Arethia retired from senior healthcare after years of service. It was an honor and a privilege to work with a segment of the senior population that had to depend on others for its care.

You can reach Arethia at: arinfrow@yahoo.com

Dreaming

Some Dream of achieving great things.

Some just dream.

Some long to soar beyond the clouds.

Some just long.

Some soar way beyond the clouds

that others just long to soar.

Some achieve the great things

that others just long for.

Our Father plants a seed in all of His children.

Water it the best that you can.

Your dreams can be achieved.

You can soar way past the clouds.

Set your sights as high as the sky.

The seed will be watered through your tears, pain, and fears,

And most of all, through faith in your Father.

He gives to all His children the seeds of greatness.

Harvest the crop in your soul.

His abundance is evident everywhere.

God will plant and cultivate His children to do great and wonderful things.

So soar, lift your wings and fly!

Who can tell you how far you can go?

Who can tell you what you can achieve?

No one can!

So soar on the wings of His love and His promise

that He will never leave you nor forsake you...

as you fly higher and higher!

Arethia and her brother and sister, Norman and Cleo